spot

MIGHTY MACHINES

LOADERS

D1472776

by Mari Schuh

AMICUS | AMICUS INK

bucket

boom

Look for these words and pictures as you read.

tires

pipe

Here comes a loader!
What can it do?

A loader scoops loads.
It lifts loads up.
It dumps loads into trucks.

See the bucket?
It scoops dirt.
It picks up rocks.

bucket

See the boom?
It is a long arm.
It moves the bucket.

boom

See the tires? They are big.
They have ridges.
They go over bumpy ground.

tires

See the pipe?
Smoke comes out.
The loader works hard.

pipe

A loader scoops snow.

It clears the street.

See it go!

See the bucket?
It scoops dirt.
It picks up rocks.

bucket

See the boom?
It is a long arm.
It moves the bucket.

boom

bucket

boom

Did you find?

tires

pipe

See the tires? They are big.
They have ridges.
They go over bumpy ground.

tires

See the pipe?
Smoke comes out.
The loader works hard.

pipe

Spot is published by Amicus and Amicus Ink
P.O. Box 1329, Mankato, MN 56002
www.amicuspublishing.us

Library of Congress Cataloging-in-Publication Data:
Names: Schuh, Mari C., 1975- author.
Title: Loaders / by Mari Schuh.
Description: Mankato, Minnesota : Amicus, 2018. | Series: Spot.
 Mighty machines | Audience: K to grade 3.
Identifiers: LCCN 2016048895 (print) | LCCN 2016050101
 (ebook) | ISBN 9781681511030 (library binding) | ISBN
 9781681522142 (pbk.) | ISBN 9781681511931 (e-book)
Subjects: LCSH: Loaders (Machines)--Juvenile literature.
Classification: LCC TL296.5 .S38 2018 (print) | LCC TL296.5
(ebook) | DDC 621.8/6--dc23
LC record available at https://lccn.loc.gov/2016048895

Printed in the United States of America

HC 10 9 8 7 6 5 4 3 2 1
PB 10 9 8 7 6 5 4 3 2 1

To Jadyn —MS

Wendy Dieker, editor
Deb Miner, series designer
Aubrey Harper, book designer
Holly Young, photo researcher

Photos by Alamy 10–11, 12–13;
Dreamstime 6–7; iStock cover, 3,
8–9; Shutterstock 1, 4–5, 14–15

LOADERS